Master

MW00941913

MOTHER MARY

Dictations through the Messenger
Tatyana Nicholaevna Mickushina
(from 2005 through 2014)

UDC 141.339=111=03.161.1
BBC 87.7+86.4
   M59

M59 Mickushina, T.N.

Mother Mary.

Masters of Wisdom. – T.N. Mickushina. –
– 2017. – 104 pages. – (Series "Masters of Wisdom").

This book continues the Masters of Wisdom series of books.

This series of books presents collections of Messages from different Masters who are most well-known to modern humanity. These Messages were transmitted through the Messenger Tatyana N. Mickushina, who has been working under the guidance of the Masters of Wisdom since 2004. Using a special method, T. N. Mickushina has received Messages from over 50 Beings of Light.

Mother Mary is the Patroness of Russia.

The Messages call for a review of the system of values and relationships in all spheres of life, to keep the consciousness in attunement with the Divine Reality; ways of raising the consciousness are given.

ISBN-13: 978-1973908289
ISBN-10: 197390828X

Contents

Mother Mary's Life on Earth

Over two millennia separate us from the times when Mother Mary walked on Earth. Today, it is hard to believe that she had an earthly life, filled with human worries, joys and sufferings. We are used to perceiving her as an Ascended Master, yet, she had worldly qualities as well. The stories and reminiscences of Mother Mary's contemporaries form a fairly visual image of her; she was of average height, had golden hair and quick eyes, her pupils were the color of a black olive, her eyebrows were curved and moderately black, her gaze was strict, but not stern; she had an elongated nose, blooming lips, tranquil voice, somewhat oblong face, long arms and fingers. Her gait was quiet, dignified, but firm; the clothing she wore was naturally colored, modest, devoid of luxury and splendor. She was short spoken, and did not allow any careless words or improper actions, so her entire appearance was the manifestation of the soul, the embodiment of purity.

Mary's contemporaries pointed out her perfect spiritual qualities. Her rule was not to insult or offend anyone, to be good-hearted to everyone, to respect the elder, not to envy those who are equal to her, to avoid boasting, to be reasonable, and to appreciate virtue.

She was never proud in front of a modest person, never laughed at the weak, and never avoided the needy. When talking to others, she carried herself respectably, did not become outraged or angry, and was completely unpretentious.

The Holy Virgin's entire life on Earth lasted 72 years, based on the calculations of the holy church fathers and authoritative ecclesiastic sources.

Luke the Evangelist, who had known Saint Virgin Mary well, wrote down several important events of her early years of life based on her words. Being a doctor and an artist, based on the legend, he created her portrait-icon, from which iconographers later made copies.

Mother Mary's parents lived in the city of Nazareth, which was three days of travel away from Jerusalem. Her father Joachim came from the line of King David [1]

---

[1] David, the first king of Judah and the third king of Israel (1055-1015 B.C. or 1010-970 B.C. according to the new chronology). In his youth, he became famous for fighting the Philistine giant Goliath. David was the progenitor of the only dynasty of Judah kings. In the Jewish legends, David was depicted as a role-model mighty king, brave warrior and spiritual poet. The authorship of Jewish religious songs, prayers and psalms is attributed to David. According to the Jewish

Her mother Anne was the youngest daughter of a priest from the line of Aaron[2] pontiff. Her elder sister Sofia had a daughter named Elisabeth, who later married priest Zechariah and became the mother of John the Baptist. Therefore, Elisabeth was Mother Mary's cousin, and John the Baptist was Jesus's second cousin by blood.

Joachim and Anne were righteous people, known for their humbleness and mercy to others. They lived until an old age and did not have children, which made them very upset. Despite their old age, they did not stop asking God to send them a child. They gave a promise: in the event that they do have a baby, they would devote him or her to serving God. Finally, on September 8th their daughter was born. She was given the name Mary.

When Mary turned three years old, her righteous parents prepared to carry out their vow: they took their daughter to the church of Jerusalem to devote her to God.

---

beliefs, the Messiah was supposed to come from the line of David (Brockhaus and Efron Encyclopedic Dictionary).

[2] **Aaron** was the first pontiff of the Jewish people and the elder brother of prophet and lawgiver Moses (Exodus 28:1).

Besides its sacred buildings, the church also had many courts and narthexes that contained various rooms for people who carried out certain sacred services. Widows and virgins who led an abstinent life, also lived in the church buildings.

Mary was left to live at the church. Under the patronage of experienced lady mentors, she and other girls learned the law of the Lord and crafts, prayed and read the Holy Scriptures. Mary had an acute mind; she liked to study and everyone admired her prudence. The crafts that she mastered included flax and wool spinning. She also liked to do silk embroidery, especially on priest's clothing for church services, and was excellent in everything she did.

Mary lived at the church for 11 years and grew up into a very righteous, modest, hard working person, who was devoted to God in every way. Willing to only serve God, she gave a vow not to ever get married and to stay a Virgin for the rest of her life.

According to the law that existed at the time, Mary could no longer stay at the church, and was supposed to get married. In order to obey the marriage law, priest Zechariah, who knew and respected her vow, formally got her engaged to a remote relative, an 80-year old widower Joseph.[3] Joseph gave a promise to take care of Mary and safeguard her virginity. Joseph lived in the town of Nazareth. He also came from the royal family of King David, but was not rich and worked as a carpenter. From the few stories about Joseph in the Holy Scriptures, it is obvious that he had a mature character: he was quite firm in his aspirations to the Holy, determined, high-hearted, sincere, modest, pure, peaceable, attentive to the voice of his conscience and decrees from above. Joseph had children from his first marriage: four sons, who are called Jesus's "brothers" in the testaments, and two daughters. One of the daughters, Mary, lived in her father's house. When Virgin Mary, after getting engaged with Joseph, came to his home, she became friends with his daughter and treated her like her sister.

According to the story, in Joseph's house, Virgin Mary received the Glad Tidings from Archangel Gabriel, that the Lord had chosen her to be the Mother of the world's Savior.

In the book "Human aura" dictated through the messengers Mark and Elizabeth Profet, explains the essence of immaculate conception:

---

[3] Joseph (incarnation of Saint Germain) was sent to be the patron and protector of Mary and Jesus.

«When the Holy Spirit came upon the virgin consciousness of Mary, who embodied the ray of the Mother, and the power of the Supreme Lord entered her being, the energies of Alpha and Omega merged in her womb in order to fulfill the promise of the coming of the Messiah. By being devoted to the Ray of the Mother and by the immaculate image of Christ's soul, she magnetized a powerful focus of the Omega polarity in her four lower bodies and chakras.

The realization of God as a Mother was so real in Mary's consciousness, and her identification with the Mother flame was so full, that in the true meaning of her "self" as God she became God's realization of Himself as a Mother on the material plane. Hence Gabriel's greeting: "Rejoice Blessed Mary, the Lord is with You! Blessed are You among women».

This event took place during the sixth month after Archangel Gabriel's visit to priest Zechariah about the birth of his son – the future Prophet John the Baptist[4].

The year of Jesus's birth could not be determined exactly even in those ages due to various changes in time tracking. In the Gospel according to St. Luke, it is said that, before Christ was born, the emperor had ordered that a census of the population be held. In the Jewish tradition, the census was done by the tribes and clans, each of which had certain towns and ancestral homes where they were to be registered. David's place of birth was Bethlehem. Therefore, Joseph and Mary, as David's descendants, had to travel there to participate in the census. The town was small and overfilled with people who came to register in the census. As none of the houses had any space for them, Joseph and

---

[4] Mother Mary and her sister Elizabeth developed an educational system for John the Baptist and Jesus when the latter were still children. This system is now known as the Montessori Method (from the book The Masters and Their Retreats).

Mary had to find shelter in the surrounding area. Close to the Bethlehem gates, there was a cave in a rocky mountain, where the shepherds put cattle during storms or escaped from extreme heat in the summer. There was a hollow in one of the cave walls which served as a crib for cattle. Mary and Joseph had no choice but to use that manger as a shelter. That is where the Holy Virgin delivered Jesus on the 25th of December, painlessly, without anybody else's help.

Even before the birth of the Messiah was revealed in Judea, it was known about in the East. The Three Wise Men[5] of the East, led by the Star of Bethlehem, came to the birth place of Jesus to greet him and to bring the poor family some material aid. Would they expect to find the Baby Jesus and His Mother "amidst camel waste and roaring donkeys? The human mind was trying to place the future Prophet at least near a church or among majestic walls."[6]

Before dawn, the wise men put on their best clothes and went through the cote into the small dwelling next to the rock. Mother Mary with Jesus in her arms was sitting by the fire. The wise men gave her the treasures and sacred items, and warned her that she would need to travel. Herod, who was the king at that time, had been warned shortly before that he would lose his throne. Knowing the prophecy, that the "new King of Judea"

---

[5] Those Three Wise Men were El Morya, Kuthumi and Djwal Khul.

[6] From the book The Cryptograms of the East by Helena Roerich.

was to be born soon, he made a cruel order to kill all infants in Bethlehem and the neighboring territories. Joseph and Mary took the Baby to Egypt in order to save Jesus from Herod's evil plan.

After returning from Egypt, the family settled in Nazareth again. Joseph continued his carpentry work, "feeding with the work of his hands." As he grew, Jesus shared the work with Joseph so eagerly that people called him not only the carpenter's son, but also simply the carpenter.

Mother Mary's life was spent on the same activities with the same humility and piety as before. There is a legend, according to which, she taught reading and writing to children of both genders, diligently served the

poor, gave donations, and took care of the sick and helped orphans and widows. She was tireless in her crafts as before and performed them with care, making clothes for herself and for her son. Later, among other activities, Mother Mary wove a seamless red robe, which was wonderfully made and which served Jesus as his permanent clothes.

Mother Mary saw Her son off on the road when He went to wander in order to gain knowledge. And when Jesus returned to fulfill His service for the next three years, Mother Mary carried Her service alongside Her son. This time became a great challenge for Mary. These years of her life, are known mostly through the prism of the events that happened in the life of her son. Because of his love and faith, Mary always wanted to be as close to Jesus as possible during his endless travels. Near Pilate's house, under the arch, a small ditch is shown in the wall, where, according to legend, Mother Mary stood during Jesus's trial. The legend adds that the Holy Virgin addressed Pilate begging him for mercy to her son when Christ's procession to the cross began. She was also present when Jesus was crucified...

After Jesus's ascension, Mother Mary gathered disciples and friends and formed a colony in Bethany,[7] where they received directions from God. Accompanied by Beloved John and five other apostles, Mother Mary visited various places around the world. First, they went to Luxor in Egypt, and then they traveled across the Mediterranean Sea to the island of Crete. They crossed the Strait of Gibraltar, stopped in Fatima in Portugal, Lourdes in Southern France, Glastonbury on the British Islands, and Ireland to prepare the path for those who would come after her to expand the Christ-Consciousness. Those visits set the foundation for Apostle Paul's work in Greece and Mother Mary's appearances in Fatima and Lourdes. They motivated King Arthur to found the order of the Knights of the Round Table and go on a quest for the Holy Grail. They allowed St. Patrick to bring Christianity to Ireland.

In the Teaching of Agni Yoga, it is said of the Mother of Jesus (Great Traveller) with the greatest reverence:

"History knows little about the Mother of the Great Pilgrim, who was as exceptional as Her Son. The Mother came from a great family and was the embodiment of refinement and nobility of spirit. She was the One who laid the foundation for His first high ideals, and sang a lullaby to Him in which She foretold His miraculous future. She took great care to safeguard Her Child, and was a source of strength for His great achievements.

---

[7] Bethany – is a village in Palestine near the Mount of Olives, from which Jesus made his last entry into Jerusalem.

She knew several languages, and thus made the path easier for Him. Nor did She object to His long pilgrimages, and gathered all that was necessary to make the travels easier. She rightly valued the common people and knew that they would guard the treasures of His Teaching. She recognized the grandeur of the Culmination and thus could give heart to those of diverse character who were weakened by doubt and rejection. She was prepared to experience the same achievement as Her Son, and He entrusted to Her His decision, which was confirmed by the Teachers. It was the Mother who understood the mystery of His wanderings.

In truth, very little is known about Her, but when one speaks about the Great Pilgrim one has to say a word about the Mother who led Him to the Highest." (page147 Agni Yoga)

St. John of Damascus describes how, upon the end of her outstanding life, Mary ascended from her tomb where she had been placed by the apostles after her dormition. When they opened the tomb three days later, they found nothing but twelve white lilies

From the Editors

References:

1.The Masters and Their Retreats. Mark L. Prophet and Elizabeth Clare Prophet. Summit University Press, 2003.

2.The Human Aura. Kuthumi and Djwal Kul. Summit University Press, 1996.

3.Cryptograms of the East. Helena Roerich.

4.Stories the Holy Virgin's Life on Earth with prophecies and foretypes pertaining to Her, teachings of the Church about Her, wonders and wonderworking icons of Hers. Based on the Holy Scripture, testimonies of the holy Fathers and church legends. 8th Edition. Moscow, Typo-Lithography of I. Ephremov, 1904.

5.Life of the Holy Virgin based on the books of the Menaion Reader. Compiled by Avdotya Glinka, 1904

With the help of our Love we are able to eliminate all the barriers between our worlds. And there is nothing more elevated, pleasant and blessed than the communication that we can give each other.

...

Love is capable of working miracles both in your world and ours. And Love is the very force capable of penetrating the veil.

Mother Mary
June 13, 2005

May the readings of my Rosaries become your immediate task in the near future

Mother Mary
March 26, 2005

I AM Mother Mary, your Mother in Heaven. I have come to you through this Messenger.

Many times I came through many people who are incarnated on planet Earth today. The dispensation that was granted to me lets me appear in the physical world with the help of the energy that people emanate while reading Rosaries.

I come to many people and I will have this opportunity until the stream of energy flowing from your hearts into mine is full.

I use every opportunity to appear before those who are ready to see and hear me. At present I come through Tatyana, as the time has come to set you on the right path and to tell you the words that are necessary for you at this time.

You may imagine me. I am standing right in front of you when you are reading these lines. I am standing in front of you with a bunch of roses in my hands. I have prepared this bunch for you, my beloved. For you, who aspires and spends so many hours reading my Rosaries. Do not give up this work, I ask you, my beloved.

I understand that there are many temptations and seductions in your world that seem to you to be more important than the prayers that I ask you to read for me every day.

However, if it were not necessary to ask for your service at this period of time I would not have bothered you.

Beloved, it does not matter which Rosary you read and whether you read traditional Catholic Rosaries or Rosaries I have given through many Messengers lately. I would like you to understand that only your heart's aspiration and purity, your wish to help the entire Life on this planet are of importance.

I do not want to frighten you with any forthcoming calamities and cataclysms. It is not because they are not coming in the near future. Cataclysms are inevitable, as people stubbornly do not want to keep their eyes on Heaven and go on persisting in their aspiration to get more and more pleasures of this world.

That is why the energy of your prayers is so necessary for us. I assure each of you who read my Rosaries every day at this difficult time that within 100 kilometers around the place of your reading there will be no cataclysms or calamities.

I especially appeal to the people of my favorite country, Russia. Due to the great space your country occupies and very low density of population in many regions, you are expected to give us your service with double and even triple efforts. Russia has been granted a great mission to transform mankind's consciousness and to raise this consciousness onto a higher level.

That is why I ask everyone who hears this Message — may the reading of my Rosaries, independent of the Messenger through whom these Rosaries come to you, become your intermediate task in the near future. You must give me one Rosary every day. I ask you. I beg you, my beloved.

I will come myself and give one rose from my bunch as a sign of my love to each of you who pledge to faithfully read my Rosaries every day.

And that is not everything, my beloved. I ask you to read my Rosaries with a feeling of the mightiest love you can feel towards your planet, towards all living creatures inhabiting this planet. And I ask you to descend into your heart and to feel its warmth before reading a Rosary. Think of me. I know how hard it is for you to be incarnated on Earth at this difficult time. But remember how difficult it was for me when my son Jesus was crucified before my eyes. How could I watch his sufferings?

Beloved, do you love me? Can you send me Love from your heart just for a few minutes before reading a Rosary every day? It is not difficult. Will you comply with my request?

I love all of you, and I will come to you while reading your Rosaries. You will feel; you will certainly feel my presence. You may stop reading and talk to me. I will lend my ear to all your requests and wishes.

And I promise to render you any help that the Cosmic Law will let me render.

I will do my best to help you. Can I also expect you to do what I ask you?

Believe me, if I did not know what I know and what is hidden from your eyes, I would never ask you to do the work that only you can do.

Least of all I want you to feel fear. Be afraid of nothing. I was among you; I was stepping on earth and I can assure you that each of you receives during his life as many trials as you can endure.

The karma created by mankind is too heavy. Great sacrifices and sufferings are demanded for the redemption of it.

But God is gracious and He grants you the means to soften your karma and relieve your burden. Do not scorn these means and the opportunity granted to you.

I leave you. I was happy to use this opportunity to remind you again about the work you should fulfill.

I will certainly meet with each of you while reading your everyday Rosaries.

I AM Mother Mary, and goodbye until we meet again.

The rebirth of Russia as the land of the Mother will take place very soon

Beloved Mother Mary
June 13, 2005

I AM Mother Mary, having come to you through this Messenger.

I am pleased to meet you today. I am especially glad to meet you today because many changes have taken place since our last meeting. And I thank all of you who have devoted all your free time to saying Rosaries during the whole period since our last meeting. I promised to come and to gift you a rose. I have been literally pouring roses upon many of you. And if you could notice with the eyes of your souls what is taking place around you, you would be able to see that the whole room in which you are saying the Rosaries is literally heaped with roses.

I give thanks to you. I am profoundly grateful to everybody who has answered my call. All of the energy that you have selflessly been giving to me, I have directed to create conditions in your life which

24

enable you to achieve greater awareness and greater understanding of current events.

My Love was invariably being poured upon you during your saying of the Rosaries. And I was feeling your Love. Oh, you cannot even imagine the bliss I experience while taking your Love into my heart. Your Love penetrates the veil and flows like blessed incense wrapping me. I always see clearly whose heart is sending me this Love and I can always send my blessing to your heart and your lifestream.

Blessed be all those devoted and compassionate hearts who, amid the hustle and bustle of the day, find time to stop and give me Love and the energy of the Rosary. Let us not interrupt this flow of Love and this energy exchange between our octaves.

Just imagine that each of your prayers addressed to me makes the veil between our worlds thinner and thinner. There are regions on the globe where the power of your prayers has made the communication between our worlds possible to such an extent that you can even feel me touching you and sense the aroma of the roses I am heaping upon you.

Beloved, do not interrupt your prayers.

I need your Love and prayers as before. You are aware of the important events that have taken place on Earth. And I am happy to greet those of you who have reached the next stage of the evolution of your consciousness. And I am very happy that a lot of people who have devoted their time to the saying of Rosaries have managed to rise to this higher level. The prayers about you and your relatives that I have been offering during this time have also taken effect.

Now I direct my attention to the Land of the Mother — Russia. You are aware of the fact that Russia is the country I extend special patronage to. And my presence over Russia can be intensified only if as many as possible of the sons and daughters of this country pay deference to me and give me the energy of the Rosaries.

You know that Orthodoxy does not have a tradition of saying Rosaries. Therefore, those of you who confine yourselves strictly to the Orthodox traditions can do without reading Rosaries. It is enough for you to look at my image and send me your Love, and I will always feel this. There are no restrictions in the Divine world. You yourselves invented all the restrictions by creating traditions. That is why I ask you just to give me your Love.

Do you remember Serafim Sarovsky? Can you remember him serving before my image on the icon called "Affection"? He did not even recite prayers, but his eyes filled with tears and he plunged into a totally blissful state of Love towards me. Serafim Sarovsky was one of my most devoted servants. And I still remember the moments of our commune spent together in the woods.

You cannot even imagine this inexpressible miracle given to us by the Lord. With the help of our Love we are able to eliminate all the barriers between our worlds. And there is nothing more elevated, pleasant and blessed than the communication that we can give each other.

We exist on the different sides of the border separating our worlds. However, the border itself is becoming thinner and thinner under the influence of the overmastering power of Love. There are no barriers for the power of Love, beloved.

Love is capable of working miracles both in your world and ours. And Love is the very force capable of penetrating the veil.

When you have a minute to leave your bustle and go before my image, please do not think that I am somewhere far away. I hear the sincere call of your heart. I am where you are. I hear every word you say to me, no matter whether you pronounce these words aloud or just within your heart.

And if you bate your breath and look narrowly, you can even spot my presence next to you in the shape of a light, subtle cloud. You can also sense a dainty aroma of the roses or feel me touching you.

I love watching your faces during your prayers. And sometimes I allow myself to approach you while you are saying the Rosaries and to kiss or stroke you.

You, many of you, feel my touches and even try to drive me away like an annoying fly. Oh, if you only admitted in your consciousness a thought that it was not a fly but Mother Mary herself who came to kiss you. You would feel very awkward and funny.

Our worlds are much closer to each other than you can imagine. And even now you can feel my presence during your prayers. There is no closer Master than me for the people of Earth. I answer literally all your requests. And I am very sorry that at times your karma is so heavy that I cannot give you the help you ask me for. However, nothing is impossible for God. And after you have realized your past mistakes at the new level, it is possible that the decision of the Karmic Board will be altered and I will be allowed to help you.

I am very happy that for the first time during the last 100 years I have a chance to be present more and more often in the land of Russia — in my land, the land I extend special patronage to. Therefore, do not be despondent. All your prayers are being heard and the rescue is racing to the land of Russia. This rescue will come in a very short time according to the cosmic measures. Everything will change. And the rebirth of Russia as the land of the Mother will take place very soon.

Meanwhile I ask you not to stop the wheel of prayers. And if due to your stirring life you cannot dedicate much time to prayers, I think you can always find time and a chance amid the bustle of the day to cast a look at my image or an icon and give me your Love.

It will take mere seconds. But if you are able to send me your Love just a few times during a day, this will substitute for the saying of the Rosaries and the reading of prayers.

Always have my image with you. Keep my image in your handbag or in an amulet. Always remember that there in the physical world where my focus is, I can establish my presence owing to the energy of Love that you send me.

Please be patient, beloved. It is not too long to wait. Come out at dawn and feel the delightful moment when the Sun is still below the horizon, but everybody around is already anticipating the instant of the sunrise. And right now the whole world is at the point of expecting the rise of the Sun — the Sun of Faith, the Sun of Love, and the Sun of Hope.

The sunrise of your consciousness is as inevitable as the rise of the Sun foreseen by your being.

I AM Mother Mary, always loving you and waiting for our meeting.

About the spiritual mission of Russia

Beloved Mother Mary
June 25, 2007

I AM Mother Mary, who has come to you on this day. I am so glad that the Divine opportunity for our association with you has continued. I am so glad to come to you again for the talk.

Oh, if you could only know how much I would like to tell you. If you do not object, I will begin with the most important topic. I will begin with the new Divine mercy that has been granted during these very days at the Karmic Board session that is taking place now.

I cannot wait to bring joyous news to you! You know that I am the patron of Russia, and you also know that the people of this country have been giving their attention to me in their prayers since the old times. I help to heal. My icons have wonderworking power; they protect and heal those who need to be protected and healed.

I put my presence in many of my icons. You can always obtain answers to the questions that are troubling you by looking at my facial expression and into my eyes on the icon. I strive to associate with you and I help you as much as I can, my beloved children.

I have just returned from the Karmic Board session. That joyous news that I would like to tell you concerns my beloved Russia. You know that a big mission is awaiting that country — the mission to lead people along the spiritual Path. The path has finally opened up and Russia has come to a point on its path where its future mission is already visible. Russia has reached the point that presupposes the uncovering of the mission.

You know that many prophets of the past spoke about the great role and mission of this country. However, in practice, everything went the opposite way. The image of Russia that has formed in the past few decades in the West is not very attractive.

We carefully observed the development of those individuals whose fates are connected with Russia and who have been incarnating in Russia for many centuries. You know, we made a conclusion that thanks to its best representatives, Russia has earned the right to step on the Path of the spiritual leader of the world. I ask that you do not confuse this role and this mission with the role that — not so long ago — the entire world assigned to Russia, or the Soviet Union, as it was called at that time.

In a way, the current role is a direct opposite of the mission that it had taken on earlier. The difference is that Russia is meant to become a highly spiritual country. It is at this time, despite the seeming lack of spirituality, that the foundation of the future spiritual country is created. It is at this time that the people of Russia who are tired of despair and lack of faith are ready to turn to the source of the Divine goodness, to come down on their knees and say inside their hearts:

"**Lord, forgive me, Lord, forgive us, Heavenly Father. We did not know what we were doing. We relied on our flesh, and we created many woes due to our foolishness. Lord, please, answer our prayer. Forgive us, O Lord, for everything that we have done, for all the woes and misfortunes that we have brought to the world. Lord, if it be Your Will, come to our country, enlighten us, and help us follow Your Path.**"

After the people of Russia, represented by its best sons and daughters, repent in their hearts, then an unprecedented Divine opportunity will open up for that country.

You will soon face a tremendous explosion of spirituality in Russia. It will not matter to you which temple to visit and at which temple you kneel. That is because in your consciousness, you will rise to the Divine top from which you will no longer see the former contradictions between different faiths and religions. Your hearts will become filled with such Divine goodness that you will stop experiencing any negative reactions toward your neighbors who are different from you. You should unite in the longing of your hearts. You should unite with the motto of spiritual unity of the nation. Only after repentance is the spiritual unity possible. Only after spiritual unity will Russia become capable of settling down to the physical plane the models of spiritual creations of the best representatives of mankind, which are now established in the subtle plane and are ready to come down to the physical plane.

I need to tell you that the future of Russia is not related to the adherence to a certain faith, but to the tolerance of any true manifestation of worship of God. I am not talking about the manifestations of faith intolerance that took place in the past. I am talking about a new level of consciousness of a different quality that will embrace the Divinity and smooth out all the contradictions that the sly human mind has been purposefully exacerbating over the past millennia.

I have come to you on this day to bring to your consciousness the need to understand the mission of Russia. I have not come for you to be proud, but for you to lift your spirits and be able to rise to the new stage of development.

Night, the dark night is over for Russia. Come outside at dawn and watch the sunrise. In the same way, the sun of the Divine consciousness has started to rise in the people of Russia.

Stop looking back at the West. Stop taking the models that are not only useless but also harmful. Your mission is to bring new models. Very soon, the people of the entire world will be surprised to listen to and look at the changes that will be taking place in Russia. The changes in this country will not come from those in power, from politicians or economists. The changes will come from the people's hearts, and those changes will be impossible to miss.

Every time you look into the eyes of the little human beings who have come into incarnation again, try to understand the message that those eyes contain.

Your responsibility is not only to help the new generation to receive everything necessary on the material plane. Your task is also to provide assistance to each of the newly incarnated people to fulfill their Divine purpose.

It is at this time that the individuals who will make Russia the spiritual capital of the world have begun to incarnate. Do not miss your opportunity of world service. Help these children of Earth, the representatives of the new Race.

Now I am ready to begin the Blessing. I have come on this day to give you a part of my heart, to give Heavenly goodness to those of you who are reading my Message. I have come to give you the entire momentum of my Love, Faith, and Hope.

I am asking you to do one thing: Never forget your Divine origin and your Divine purpose in the midst of your everyday matters.

I love you with all my heart, and I am ready to come at your first call to help those who are in need.

I AM Mother Mary, who was with you on this day.

I have come today to remind you that I am always with you like a loving and caring Mother

Mother Mary
December 8, 2007

I AM Mother Mary, having come to you this day through Tatyana.

I have come to remind you once again of the opportunity that is given to you each year.

I repeat to you that every year on the 8th of December from noon to 1 p.m. local time, you can devote your time to communicate with me. I will accept any manifestation of your Love and gratitude. I will be with you throughout this Hour of Grace.

You can communicate with me and see me.

It would be as if I were beside you. I use the energy given by you in order to manifest my presence everywhere on Earth simultaneously. The purer your aspiration is, the stronger my presence beside you will be. And that is how we will be able to raise the vibrations of the physical plane every year.

In turn, God gives you an opportunity to ask me about manifesting your wishes concerning you or your relatives.

You can ask about the manifestation of all your desires, even those that seem impossible to be realized. I will accept all your wishes in my heart and will ask God to grant your requests.

No matter what religion you belong to, you are all my children. And I will take care of you and will try to satisfy your needs and meet your requirements.

You only need to spare me one hour a year of your time.

You can listen to or sing songs dedicated to me; you can read Rosaries and prayers dedicated to me.

The impulse of your hearts, directed to me, will induce me to hear you, and I will make every effort to realize your requests. The energy of prayer and Love given by you is not always enough to realize your request.

That is why I will be highly grateful to you if you can think about me more often and send me your energy of Love and prayer.

When a difficult situation occurs in your life, it is a signal that you haven't turned to me in a long time, and I was not able to resolve the situation and direct its course to the easiest way.

Always remember that God does not want to punish you. He wants you to follow the Path of Love. If you do bad things like small children, do not forget to repent of them sincerely and ask me for help so that the mistakes you have made do not cause a severe retribution, because the Law requires that all your deeds and their energy should be returned to you. Then you will be able to see your own mistakes and take measures to correct them.

No matter how many times you make mistakes, it is important that you constantly strive for righteousness and correct the mistakes that you made.

With your human consciousness you cannot estimate to what extent the things that you do are bad or good in God's eyes; therefore, ask the Heavens for help more often. Ask for the atonement of your sins.

Sometimes a person performs a terrible deed in the eyes of society; however, in God's eyes, this deed is not a sin because the person is being used by God as a tool so that someone can expiate his karma.

That is why it is said that you do not judge. Judge not and you will not be judged.

However, you should never tolerate the actions of those individuals who have forgotten themselves in play and have committed unseemly deeds expecting that God will forgive them for everything.

God is perfectly merciful and patient, but when a person doesn't want to learn lessons from his own behavior, then he creates a very difficult situation for himself. According to the extent that a person can be humble under the circumstances he has gotten himself into, God judges the sincerity and repentance of the person.

Remember, every time you face a heavy and unfair situation in your life, from your point of view, in 100 percent of the cases you alone were the reason for creating this situation, thanks to your wrong choices and bad deeds.

Everything in your life is determined by your past choices and deeds.

But there isn't any predetermination in your destiny, because sometimes one correct choice of yours and a righteous deed expiates the karma of many sins, including the most terrible ones, committed by you in the past.

I have come today to remind you that I am always with you like a loving and caring Mother.

I love all of you, my children, and I care about you.

Live in peace and Love.

I AM Mother Mary.

Every time I come, I feel more and more confident on Earth

Mother Mary
December 21, 2007

I AM Mother Mary, having come to you again. The fragrance of roses accompanies my visit to you.

You do not notice our presence near you or the signs that we tirelessly give you. However, there is something that becomes evident and is impossible to hide, even from the consciousness of those individuals who are far from being interested in any kind of religion, in the Teaching of the Ascended Masters, or in any other new-fashioned teachings and movements. This is manifesting in ordinary life. Suddenly you raise your head and find a sign from our world in your everyday vanity. Or you suddenly find yourself at some unknown place, and you try to remember why it is familiar to you. You have never been there before. However, this place is painfully familiar to you. And you suddenly begin to remember an article you have read about past incarnations, and it gives you the shivers because you have remembered this place, and you have even had the pictures of your previous life flash before your eyes.

Even if you do not believe in any mysticism, at times you are afraid to admit that you have had a contact with the finer world.

You see, my beloved, how close our worlds are. And you see, my beloved, how much they have approached each other over the past few years.

You know that I come to many people. It happens thanks to the infinite grace of God. He gives me this opportunity because the people of Earth need constant signs and constant reminding that there is another world, the higher one, where the souls of the best representatives of humanity aspire.

As soon as you start thinking of our world, you will certainly begin to notice our Messages that we leave here and there, even among your things.

Have you ever tried to speak with angels? Have you ever asked angels to help you find the things that you have lost? Try to get in touch with them. Now, as never before, is a very special time before Christmas when miracles become more real.

I have come to you today and brought you my mood, my lightness, and my tender Love that overfills my heart.

You cannot imagine how happy I am that at last I can come to the land of Russia through our Messenger and give my Messages through her.

You cannot imagine how significant this victory of Heavens is, to feel your recognition of our Messenger. This recognition of yours has manifested on the physical plane as the house for work and meditation; and on the finer plane your recognition has turned into a Divine opportunity that we have gotten for Russia and for the work in the land of Russia.

All the efforts you apply are never lost. Imagine the angels who gather every particle of your energy of Love and Gratitude that you send to the Heavens. They gather whole storages of your energy by the end of a year, and during the annual session at the end of the year, which has already begun, the Karmic Board has a chance to direct your energy and give new dispensations and new opportunities to humankind of Earth.

I have come to you today to thank you for the work you have done this year. I am especially grateful to those souls who have tirelessly read Rosaries for the whole year; and I thank all of you because I have an opportunity to use the energy of Love that I have received to help humankind of Earth.

Ask me for help in your prayers. I have the opportunity to help you. I do it with pleasure when your karma allows the help to be rendered. However, in especially serious cases, additional energy is needed. I am very glad that your prayers, which you have sent to me during the Hour of Mercy on the 8th of December, have allowed me to help many souls.

I thank you.

Now, at the end of the year, all the energy of your prayers and all the energy of your Love that you send to Mother Earth and to us, the Ascended Hosts, will be used for the new dispensations for the development of our mission on Earth, according to the decision of the Karmic Board. We hope that with your help and with the help of our Messenger we will manage to create a new focus of Light and to spread the effect of this focus around the whole planet Earth.

I have come at this dark period of the year in the western hemisphere. Still, I hope that as spring inevitably comes after this dark time of the year, the spring of human consciousness will also come; and the door, through which the Light of Heavens will penetrate into the world of each of you, will open in the heart of every man incarnated on Earth at this difficult time.

I hope for it; and every time I come I feel more and more confident on Earth because your Love and devotion allow me to be present among you and to give tangible help. O, there is no greater pleasure for me than to give help to those who need it when I am able to do that.

Spare no energy of your prayers and spare no Love of yours, which you send to everything around you. Every particle of the energy you send is carefully saved, and it is used for the good of the evolutions of planet Earth.

Now the time has come for us to part. However, I hope that I will be allowed to come to you again and again through Tatyana. Many Masters also wish to come in contact with you through the heart of our Messenger and to give you their instructions, their energy, and their Love!

Many Ascended Masters need contact with humankind of Earth. Thanks to that contact, the Ascended Hosts are more successful in fulfilling the tasks that must be fulfilled on Earth in the nearest future.

I am leaving you, and to say goodbye I am sending you all the Love of my heart.

Your Mother Mary, with Love toward you.

Recommendations at the end of the year

Beloved Mother Mary
December 27, 2007

I AM your Mother Mary, having come in order to give this Message.

I have come on one of the last days of this year in order to sum up some results and to outline the future guidelines in your consciousness.

I have come to talk to you without any hurry — sincerely — carefully, and gently.

I have come as a loving and careful mother. Indeed, I am your mother for I do care about you and heal your souls. When it is especially hard for you, all of you come to me.

I know that it is hard for you. I know that you are at the meeting, the crossing of the new energies coming into your world and the old energies that are still prevailing in your world. It is always very hard to live at a transitional time. Your physical bodies and your finer conductors sometimes cannot cope with the increased load. However, you should put up with it. There is no other way. Along with me, many angel-healers and many Masters are ready to give you all feasible and possible help. Therefore, do not ignore the help that the Heavens are giving to you. Turn for help to the Masters, the angels, the elementals, and to me personally.

I am carrying the burden of many incarnated sons and daughters of God. I am trying to ease your fate. However, you also can help me. I need your energy, your prayers, and your Love.

We can and should help each other. I will ease your burden at this transitional time, and you give me an additional reserve of energy, please.

I am listening to your prayers; and sometimes only one prayer sincerely read in your heart is enough to render help. However, you do not find time to send me the energy of your prayer. I cannot give you help when you demand help from me. I can only help humble hearts, the hearts that have repented and are ready to obey any of our requirements.

As always, we are calling you to the right state of your consciousness. Some people need fasting, prayer, repentance, confession, and communion in order to achieve the right state of consciousness.

The sincere tears of repentance are enough for the others. Washed by those tears in the morning after the sleepless night, my precious children are capable of sincere prayer, and the extent of repentance present in their hearts gives me an opportunity to render the help they need.

I see your suffering. I feel compassion toward you. However, you should understand me. There are some kinds of karma from your past deeds that can be expiated only by suffering.

There is a lot of grief and suffering in your world.

I see it. I also see other things. I see how the young people use the precious energy of Love completely irresponsibly. I see... and my heart stops with a shudder because I know what suffering those souls will be subjected to in the future. You doom yourselves to much suffering.

I have come to remind you of the responsibility for your actions so that you do not ask me for deliverance from suffering and for healing when your life is over, and you are burdened with the heavy baggage of illnesses and psychological problems. I would like young people to ask for my help, advice, and support right now so that in their mature age they can serve for the Glory of God and perform Divine deeds on the physical plane.

You all are obliged to direct your eyes at the young people. Those who are at the end of life and have finally realized the Divine Truth more or less, you can pass your experience to the new generation. Think about the way in which you can do that — it is necessary to do it, I am telling you.

I care about the future generation because I foresee big changes soon, especially in my favorite Russia.

Extensive work and huge responsibility will lie upon the very youth who wander about the streets and do not know what to do. Therefore, I ask you not to ignore your duty. Let the young people receive the knowledge of the Divine Law existing in this universe. Let that knowledge reach the young hearts. It is not necessary to use the institution of the church in order to make the young fulfill the directions of one or another religion. It is not necessary at all. It is important that God settles in the heart of every human living in the world. It is important that every human lives in accordance with the Law.

If you think that church ceremonies have become old and alienate the young, then give them a codex of moral norms and rules in the form of lectures, films, or seminars. Give the young the right guidelines for their lives. This is your duty, the duty of everyone who is reading this Message of mine now.

I have come to you on this day at the end of the year because this time at the end of the year and the sense of the New Year is disposed to consideration. Try to follow the inner need of reflection in your heart. Try to stay alone. Your friends and acquaintances and all the existing traditions will be telling you the opposite and will be urging you to join a noisy party and traditional New Year's and Christmas table.

Do not rush to noisy companies. Do not create new karma to untangle for the entire next year. At the end of the next year, do not complain to me that it is hard for you and that you lack health and energy.

Follow the pieces of advice that I give you year after year, and every successive year will be happier than the previous one.

May God help you during the New Year!

I AM Mother Mary, and I have been with you on this day.

Heart to heart talk

Mother Mary
January 4, 2009

I AM Mother Mary, coming to you again, as usual, for a heart-to-heart talk. When hearts are talking, minds are silent. And true communication between us becomes possible only when we establish contact at the level of our hearts.

You lack for Love. You lack for Light. You are sometimes nearly out of breath due to insufficiency of Divine energy as if it were a lack of oxygen.

You should spend more time speaking heart-to-heart with me.

I am ready to listen to all your complaints and requests. Do not feel shy. I know that men are particularly shy to show their feelings. And when a special moment of our communication comes, in confusion they brush away a tear welled up in their eyes.

Feel free to weep. Your soul is yearning for true communication. You are seeking for and still fail to find an ideal in your world, both men and women. You focus on your bodies, but true Love shows itself at the level of your souls and even at the level of your Higher Self.

Do not feel embarrassed when your eyes are misted over with tears during our communication. You committed actions that were not very good toward women, your mothers, and sisters many times in your past lives and during this life. May your misdeeds get dissolved in the tears, and negative energies leave you forever.

Your repentance, though you may not even realize that it is repentance, opens a new opportunity for you: a New view of the world.

Do not feel embarrassed about your tears. They carry away the karma created by your ignorance or by your lack of wisdom.

I am with you. I am always with you, and you can always turn to me for help at a hard moment of your life.

I am nearer to the physical plane of planet Earth than all of the Masters. It is my special mission. I guard your homes and your country. I am ready to come to you at your first call.

And it all becomes possible thanks to your efforts, thanks to that energy of Love and prayer that I receive from you.

The Rosaries that you dedicate to me give me an opportunity to render help for many souls seeking help.

I always know when you read the Rosary from the bottom of your heart. A stream of energy flows between us: an upward one from you and a downward one from me. That is how you get my energy of Love and Mercy.

When you are especially sad and you do not have any energy to read a Rosary, you can just think about me, listen to melodies dedicated to me. And then the flow of energy from you reaches me as well, and I feel you, each of you. By the grace of God I feel each of His sons and daughters at the moment when they think about me or turn to me for help.

So today you can use the opportunity granted by Heaven and ask me for help and support in your hour of need as before.

Beloved Jesus told you yesterday that I had set my presence in many images of mine. And you can feel it yourself. Some icons of me have a miracle-working effect. And sometimes it is enough for you just to visualize one of the icons to receive my ray of support.

When I have an opportunity to be present among you, and it is not a secret that God gives me such a mercy, you may not notice my presence beside you. But I am capable of being present exactly where you are. It is important for me that you are staying in the atmosphere of peace and tranquility. I come invisible and unnoticeable, and only by a slight fragrance of roses accompanying my appearance you can occasionally guess that I have visited you.

I have come on this winter day with the news that, I hope, you will find useful. I would like to give you a prayer to the Most Holy Mother of God for your prayer hour:

"In the name of I AM THAT I AM, Most Holy Mother of God, beloved Mother Mary, I pray on bended knee to you. Words fail me to express the depth of Love in my heart that I feel toward you. Please accept my Love and gratitude. You know what is most important for the growth of my soul at present. I am asking for your help and support. I ask you to help me to not forget in the midst of the hustle of the day about those quiet minutes of our commune, which my soul remembers.

May my unbreakable bond with you support me in my life and help me to not forget about the Higher Path that I intend to follow in this life."

I sincerely hope that you will be able to be with me more often and to address me. Any of our communication, even a glance at my image, will help you to keep your consciousness at the level that makes impossible the attacks of those who have not found the way to my heart yet and are not aware of what they are doing.

I AM Mother Mary, having been with you on this day.

I invoke your consciousness Heavenward

Beloved Mother Mary
July 9, 2009

I AM Mother Mary, having come to you.

Since the time of our last meeting, events have occurred that have postponed the advent of the New Age that is still expected to come to Russia.

We have encountered resistance on the part of the opposing forces that skillfully manipulate some individuals and act through them.

I have always sought to strengthen my presence in Russia. And I am vexed by everything that is taking place.

I am not saying that everything is bad. I do hope that everything will go well. But you need to channel your energies. You need to maintain a certain level of effort every day to reach those blessed times that are to come to Russia.

I have begun my Message on a sad note. But you yourselves feel that not all is as we would like it to be, and I will add, not the way it was conceived.

However, we will not wait and let the grass grow under our feet.

If I ask you to double and triple your efforts, will you respond to my call?

For some people this will mean an intensification of their prayer efforts, and others will take up the implementation of concrete actions in the physical plane.

You can do a lot. If you regularly heed the advice that we give you and listen to the soft voice that makes its way from your heart through the hustle of your day, then we will be able to do very much and in the shortest possible time.

Now it is necessary to gather all forces for the decisive dash. Right now it is being decided whether the expected changes will come and how fast they can come, first to Russia and then to the whole world.

I will not let you in on the details, and it is not my place to show someone which steps he or she should take. Everyone should do his or her own job. And I am running my ministry day and night continually in the Higher plane.

I am as close to the earthly plane as it is possible to be. Every day I listen to all your requests and even the reproaches that you send to me.

I am ready to hear from you, even the not very pleasant things that you sometimes tell me. At times, in order for you to realize something, you must hear it yourselves. And when you are saying it to me, you hear it yourselves. The problems of many of your embodiments have stuck deep inside you.

You come up to my image and start your inner monologue. It never occurs to you that I hear every single word you are saying. And when the Divine opportunity permits, I immediately send angels to help you. The help comes immediately in the Higher plane. And a certain time is necessary for this help to materialize in your physical plane. But sometimes you do not wait long enough for this help to come and send me your reproaches and express your dissatisfaction. And immediately the flow of Divine opportunity stops. And the next time you come up to my image repenting and weeping, I render my help to you again. But then everything recurs. And when you ask about one and the same thing for the fifth or seventh time, then I do not hurry to help you, because you have not realized the whole responsibility with which you burden the angelic hosts by each of your requests.

Be consistent in your requests and actions.

Sometimes your karma does not let me intervene into your destiny, but you ask me for help every day, many times a day, for a year or even longer. And then your effort and aspiration break the invisible barrier, and help flows into your being and into your life as an extensive stream.

55

Divine mercy does not know limits. The help will come from the Higher plane. Learn to use this help. Do not cut the Divine opportunity with your negative outbursts. If you could keep attunement with the Divine world most of the time, how much easier it would be for us to render help to you and how much more successfully we could progress in the transformation of the physical plane of planet Earth.

Every time you lose equilibrium, you are like a small volcano. Everything around you begins shaking, and elemental life longs to move away from you because your vibrations do not let elemental beings come near you.

When you turn on loud music with broken rhythms, elementals and angelic beings flee headlong from the area where this awful music can be heard. The equilibrium is disrupted to such an extent that none of the beings whose responsibility it is to restore order in the Higher plane can, for a few days, enter the area where the music was played. Since you turn on music every day, your towns and settlements are like deserts now because all the inhabitants of the Higher plane have left these deserts and cannot help you.

We help you mostly through the elemental kingdom, through the elements of air, fire, water, and earth. With your behavior you deprive us of an opportunity to give you a helping hand.

We need to have a harmonious atmosphere in the physical plane. And in those places on Earth where an atmosphere of peace and balance still reigns, you are healed even when you simply get into such places.

Thousands of beings of elemental life are ready to render healing and help to you.

So think: Hasn't the time come already to return to the harmony between all the kingdoms of nature that reigned in days gone by when people were happy and felt the joy of simply being? At that time they saw elemental life and angels, and this was as natural as it is now for you to see dogs, cats, and birds.

I invoke your consciousness Heavenward. I am trying to bring home to you the fact that you live in a cage and that you have imprisoned yourselves with your own hands and have put this cage in the desert of your cities.

The time is ripe to reconsider the whole system of values and all the relationships in all the spheres of life. How is it possible to convey to you that you live in inhuman conditions?

Be brave to give up your affection to the "blessings" of your civilization, and you will gain genuine blessings and lasting values.

Nature abhors a vacuum, and each of your negative qualities will be replaced by a Divine one, and your human affections will be replaced by a state of Divine peace, harmony, tranquility, happiness, and joy. And this is exactly what you lack in your lives.

Today I have tried to direct your eyes higher than your habitual horizon to enable you to see the heights you should be aiming for now.

I AM Mother Mary.

Manifestation of Faith and Piety is necessary everywhere

Mother Mary
December 27, 2009

Beloved, I have come to you again!

I AM Mother Mary. I wish I could have come earlier, but I could not. I have a lot of work now, at the end of the year. Many people need my help and turn to me for help.

I am always ready to render help, but I have to refuse more and more often. I worry very much about this. Believe me; I use every opportunity, even the smallest ones, if the Divine opportunity is still open for the person seeking my help. But I see more and more often as the light of a soul goes out within a person, the chakras turn into holes in space. The person is already dead even though he can talk and even walk. This is a dreadful sight, beloved. Only the physical body exists, the flesh, but the soul of the person is dying.

You should take care not only of your physical body but also of your souls. Complaints and moans fill the space around Earth. Souls are suffering. I know that many souls are suffering, but simultaneously with this suffering, they are purified. When a soul is alive, there is hope that a human will live. Your souls need help. And I am not the only one who can give that help to your souls.

You also can help yourselves.

The best remedy for your souls will be sincere repentance for all the mistakes and sins that you have committed and a strong desire not to repeat those mistakes in the future. Prayer, even prayer without words, as a reconciliation with the Divine world, is capable of healing many wounds of the soul.

I know many people who are ashamed to pray; they hesitate to show their feelings. Beloved, my son Jesus taught not to pray in public for show, but at difficult moments He turned to God for help Himself.

You should do the same thing. Consonance with the Divine world, even for a short period of time during the day, allows your soul to taste the food that is so necessary for it. Your soul is nourished on Divine grace, and you are obliged to pay attention to your soul. Not so much time is needed for that, beloved.

I was astonished by the manifestation of people's Faith during the Hour of Mercy this year. So many people turned to me not only for help, but they also sincerely gave me the energy of their prayers so that I could use this energy according to my discretion.

Thank you, beloved. Thanks to your prayer efforts and diligence, I managed to give help to many souls. Many souls were healed.

I am pleased that so many wonderful souls were found on Earth who wished to share their energy with their brothers and sisters!

I would like this to happen every day, beloved! What prevents you from devoting one hour per day to sincere prayer and communication with me in your heart?

I know many people who are ashamed to pray, but they listen to songs dedicated to me at home, or at work, or in their cars. And they immerse in the magical world of melody and start a quiet communication with me in their hearts. Many people constantly carry my image with them. And when you secretly take my image and kiss it, I have a chance to know about that moment. And I immediately manifest my presence beside you.

Yes, beloved, God gave me the opportunity to manifest my presence in many places on Earth simultaneously. And where people remember me and love me, there is always a special atmosphere of protection. I am a defender of space. And very few troubles happen at those places on Earth where I can be present.

If you could constantly maintain the consonance with my heart, then you and your loved ones and all the people who live near you would be protected.

Now, I would like to dwell on another thing. And this is connected with Russia as a country to which I give my special patronage. And here I cannot tell you anything consoling. I am sad. The huge potential of this country remains dormant, in a sleeping state, as before. The Russian bogatyrs[8] sleep deeply.

Many of them go through their transition without waking up. People whose mission it was to serve as bells, whose ringing would clear the space of everything dark and ungracious, are leaving the physical plane one after another.

I would like to give my special mercy to those who are in incarnation now and perform their ministry quietly and unnoticeably for the benefit of the evolutions of Earth. There are only a few of you, but the space around you is being purified as if from ringing bells because you are capable of cleaning the space around you with your pure thoughts, selflessness, and Service.

I am granting the opportunity of a special connection with me as my gift to you. For you, I am always beside you. I know all the places in Russia where you live. And I will keep my presence constantly beside you. Thus, we will be able to multiply our efforts to purify the space.

However, for those who are skeptical about me and about the Teaching that other Masters and I are giving, I have to make a special deviation. Neither the Masters nor you can change anything in your country unless the doubt in your souls gives way to devotion and Faith, and you do honor to my servants.

----

[8] Epic hero in Russian folklore (Translator's footnote).

The manifestation of Faith and piety is necessary everywhere, in every town, and in every village. Only true Faith can open the Divine opportunity — not a show of faith that is worthless.

We need the universal manifestation of Faith and respect for the Higher Law, the Divine Law.

You will know when that happens because everything will start changing very quickly — literally in front of your eyes.

Now I can only rely on a few who carry on their Service, being misunderstood and even being the mockery of their encirclement. Woe is the nation that does not respect the manifestation of the true Faith and does not honor their saints.

I have given not a very joyful Message to you today. However, hope will never leave humankind while there are a few saints capable of maintaining the Divine level of consciousness.

I AM Mother Mary.

The whole mechanism of a happy life is integrated within you

Mother Mary
June 11, 2010

I AM Mother Mary, having come to you again on this day.

Many of you will remember this meeting with me for a long time because I will tell you something for your external consciousness that will give you the opportunity to remember our meetings in my abode.

Many of you, particularly those who feel a special closeness and affinity to me and who read my Rosaries, come to my abode during their nightly sleep, and I have a chance to talk to you. Although you forget our talks after you awaken, they still bring a significant support to your souls at this difficult time.

The souls of many of you cannot bear what is happening in your lives. When you come to me, you usually complain about your lives and ask me to take you back out of your incarnation. Many souls, the lightest and clearest, cannot adapt to the surrounding environment on the physical plane, and their souls remind me of the roses trampled down in the dirt. And every night when I have a chance to meet with you, I straighten your petals and wash them with my tears.

I understand your state very well. However, beloved, this is the state of the world now; the best souls feel depressed and do not wish to live while the people who are not burdened with great virtues feel wonderful in the environment around them.

Beloved, your souls have taken upon themselves the heavy burden of incarnation at this difficult time on Earth. And I can only remind you of that and tell you words of comfort and dry your tears. But you must continue to fulfill your mission. Each of you is very dear to my heart, and this special connection with me will always help you at the time when it seems to you that you do not have any energy or any possibility to bear the rudeness and ignorance around you.

At the hardest moments of your life, find the strength to get in touch with me in your mind. Just think about me, and I will manifest my presence beside you and share your burden. And you will feel relief and will be able to go further through life and completely fulfill your Service.

Your Service is to listen to mockeries of others and to bear all the rudeness that reigns around you. However, do not fall into condemnation. I, as my sister Quan Yin, teach you to show compassion to the souls of those who have fallen under the influence of illusion. The thirst for beauty, which is present in the souls of many people who cannot find beautiful models in the outer world, leads to inner discord and results in a revolt that is revealed by addictions, which are nothing more than the desire to destroy oneself.

All of you lack love and harmony. Some time ago you created your bad karma by your deeds, and now you are reaping the fruits of it. Beloved, if you can hear me now, if your souls respond to my words, please understand that all the heaviness that has fallen to your lot was created by you, by your incorrect actions in the past. That is why I cannot help telling you about the repentance and the awareness of your past sins and wrong deeds.

As soon as you can accept that you are responsible for everything that happens to you, you will choose the only correct road. If you firmly follow this path, then it will lead you out of the deadlock of dissatisfaction with your lives and of your unwillingness to live. You will feel the difference between the life around you and the life that God has commanded for you. You will be able to find those true and beautiful things that exist in the life around you, but you do not notice them because you constantly turn to where your mass media directs you.

We cannot be as loud-voiced as your mass media. Our voices are like the rustle of grass and the quiet murmur of a stream, so you have to attune your inner perception to our vibration and then we can be closer to each other. And you will regain the joy of life and the meaning of your existence. When your being is filled with Divine energy, you are happy because the Divine energy that is filling you can raise your vibrations to the most beautiful states of joy, love, inner harmony, and peace.

Unfortunately, most manifestations of your world are aimed at lowering your vibrations, and you lose the consonance with the Divine world and become unhappy.

I do everything in my power to remind you that the world is beautiful. You change your perception of the world depending on either your consonance with the Divine world or, conversely, on isolation from the Divine world.

Many things that surround you can lower your vibrations, and you become unhappy only because you have surrounded yourselves with incorrect and non-Divine models.

Of course, your consonance with the Divine world is manifested within you, in your hearts. However, you have to take care that this consonance is not interrupted by the inferior manifestations of your world. I understand that it is very difficult to live in peace in the world and not to feel its impact. When you make the choice in your hearts to keep the consonance with the Divine world, you become capable of gradually changing the surrounding environment, step by step, removing one low-grade manifestation after another.

Everything has definite vibrations, beloved. Everything is vibration. Your food has definite vibrations; your music has definite vibrations; the architecture of cities, clothing, and things that you use every day have definite vibrations. Some things carry positive vibrations and others carry negative vibrations. And sometimes one inharmonious thing can deprive you of your peace of mind and harmony.

It is especially necessary to be careful when you expose yourselves to the effect of constantly turned-on TVs and radios! You constantly expose yourselves to questionable models that deprive you of the opportunity to experience the Divine states of consciousness and the consonance with the Divine world. Everything that I am telling you is so natural but I am puzzled when you listen to me and even agree with me, but as soon as you stop reading my Message, you immediately return to your former lifestyles.

You have to follow our recommendations, and then in my abode you will not have to shed floods of tears and complain about your life.

The whole mechanism of a happy life is integrated within you. Why don't you use it?

I AM Mother Mary, having been with you today.

Together we can work the miracle that awaits Russia

Beloved Mother Mary
June 23, 2011

I AM Mother Mary.

I have come today to talk to you again, my beloved. I have come with one thought: to strengthen you in your Service. Now the time has come for those few who remain loyal to God and to me, His faithful servant, to demonstrate their faith and devotion.

The new Divine mercy allows the opportunity for Russia to continue. And you know that for me it is a special country. This is the country that I have been patronizing for many hundreds of years. And now it is the time when you can render your invaluable help to the Ascended Masters through your Service.

Beloved, I am asking you to take my words seriously. I wish that my words will enter into your hearts and stay there for all the time that you are in embodiment.

So, beloved, I have come with a request, and this request concerns your prayers. Your prayers are the help that you can give now.

Very few devoted and sincere hearts are incarnated now. The pressure on them is too high. However, muster up your strength. You will not have to wait long, beloved. We are expecting the New Day to dawn over Russia and then over the rest of the world.

In recent times in history I appeared to many Saints of the land of Russia. I begged them for help at those moments when storm clouds were gathering over the Russian land, before foreign invasions and threatening times.

You know St. Sergius of Radonezh and St. Seraphim of Sarov. But you do not know the many hundreds of other Saints who prayed at my request and gave me the energy of their prayers for protection during hard times.

Now there is no longer the protection over Russia that was obtained by prayers in those glorious times when devotees of the Spirit moved to deserts and forests to give me the energy of their prayers.

When the space is not protected by prayers then all the abomination of desolation penetrates there. You see that around you, and you do not know how to escape. You seek protection and ask for protection. But, beloved, Heavens can only give you help when it can be seen that you are also applying all your efforts and devoting your free time to prayers and prayer vigils.

The space over Russia needs protection. And all the Hosts of Heaven cannot protect you if there is no free will and aspiration on your part, if there is no effort applied from your side.

We come at your call and answer your prayers. But now is the time when you should answer my call. You must show your free will and diligence.

There cannot be an unlimited flow of mercy from the Heavens if Heaven does not see your efforts.

Many people do not know what to do and how to help in the difficult situation that has formed on the planet. I am telling you that your prayer is that simple help. There are no limitations and there cannot be any limits on prayer. Belonging to any religious denomination is not important. Your nationality is not important.

When a person prays sincerely, even the words of the prayer are not important because you elevate your consciousness to the level of the Ascended Hosts, and there is a direct energy exchange between our planes of being. And then even the most impossible thing can happen. The miracle that the people of Russia have always hoped for can occur.

Your land needs protection. Your planet needs protection. Each of you needs protection from the forces that are raging because their time is coming to an end. You do not have to wait long for more joyful times to come.

As it was in those times long ago when the Saints prayed for my land and protected it from hordes, prayer is also needed in your time.

Not many of you can devote even one hour per day to praying. And I can count on the fingers of one hand those who dedicate all their free time to praying or meditating on my image.

Beloved, God grants you the opportunity. And a very little thing is needed: to respond to my request with your daily efforts.

The power of prayer is the weapon that you can use to oppose any violence, any bloodshed, and any injustice that exists in your world.

There cannot be miracles that do not have the support of Heaven. And in your time there is an opportunity for a miracle to happen. And you can foster this miracle with the efforts of your hearts.

Stay in peace and goodness. Focus all your efforts on praying for those who are unwise and enchained by ignorance. Pray for the enlightenment of your rulers.

Even the utmost sinner can repent, and all his abilities and talents that he was wasting on sinful acts, he can direct at serving God.

Pray for the enlightenment of those people who make decisions in the fields of education and public health service. Pray for the salvation of the souls of those who have lost all sense of shame, robbing the invaluable riches of my land.

Sin and ignorance can be replaced in a flash by holiness and awakening. And the voice of God will stop them, as it stopped Paul in his time with the exclamation: "Is it hard for thee to kick against the pricks?" (Acts 26:14)

It is impossible to struggle against God. Every step that you take against God and His servants creates very heavy karma that should be worked off with suffering, blood, and sweat.

The land of Russia and its people have suffered enough.

There is a bright opportunity ahead that can be manifested.

I ask you to replace your despair with faith and aspiration.

I ask you to find in your hearts the feeling of unconditional Love that can grant salvation to many lost souls in these hard times.

I am calling you to the most elevated states of your consciousness.

Pray in the language that you can, with words that you know.

Aspire to me; and I will stay where you are praying.

Together we can accomplish the miracle that awaits Russia.

I AM your Mother Mary, and I have been with you today.

The end of darkness is coming, and only Light is ahead of you!

Beloved Mother Mary
June 25, 2012

I AM Mother Mary, having come to you today.

Today my arrival will not be as joyful as before because I am sad, and my sadness is associated with many manifestations of the opposing forces that have fettered mankind and prevented them from seeing the Divine Path.

I am monitoring young people, and I am monitoring people of a mature age, and the elderly. Each generation comes to this world for the implementation of its mission. And it is sad to watch people suffering without God, seeking God, yet failing in the twilight that has benighted the planet now.

A more blissful course of evolution is endeavoring to come into your lives. All of you are in need of manifestations of Divine energies, including the maternal energies of God that I am bringing to you.

My hope is not expiring and it cannot expire. I am seeking to manifest my presence wherever it is possible. If you go to the forest, you will see me among the trees; if you go to the field, you will see me in the sky against the clouds. If you are staring at a candle, I am with you, and you will feel my presence in the crackle of the candlewick and in the flicker of the flame.

If you have a habit of looking at my icon or my image, each time my presence becomes more perceptible and more tangible as you spend more and more time in meditation upon my image.

I am with you in your lives, and there are no barriers between us. I manifest my presence to every aspiring person, to everyone who by their Love is able to create a harmonious atmosphere in which I can manifest my presence.

Every time you think of me and appeal to me, we become closer to each other. And our communication becomes possible despite the external unfavorable circumstances, despite the stranglehold of inferior energies in your world.

I am with you against all odds. In this my Service is manifested. And every time you devote time for a prayer or a prayer vigil, I am able to multiply your efforts a thousand fold. That is how we will be able to overcome any resistance of the dark forces. And regardless of how difficult the time is for you, no matter how many manifestations of darkness and chaos furiously rage in the end, I know that all my children will sooner or later be with me.

I clearly behold the day when each of you, my beloved children, will be saved and broken free from the captivity of darkness and illusion.

I clearly behold the day when you will be able to overcome all your inferior states of consciousness and consequences of your wrong choices in the past.

I clearly behold the moment when the Divine Light will illuminate your faces, and this state of the Divine bliss will never leave you.

I am always with you in all the most difficult situations in which you find yourselves in your lives. And now, when I have managed to give you a particle of my love and care, I want to appeal to you once again.

Beloved, do not sink into despair and grief, nor give way to despondency. There is a mechanism hidden within you that will enable you to find a way out of the worst situation. A particle of God is dazzling within you. You should regularly find time during the day for your communication with God. You should continuously cultivate the feeling of the Divine within yourselves.

You need not force yourselves to pray. The prayerful state of consciousness is innate. And you should just constantly remember our consonance and our Oneness. Then, when you think of me, you are already taking a step closer to God.

You should find more time during the day for your communication with God. When God is able to be continually present near you wherever you are — outside, at work, at home, in a store — everything will start changing around you, and your life will change its course and aim to follow the Divine Path of development.

Not much effort is required, beloved. I insist that you should constantly keep your consciousness in consonance with the Divine Reality. Use the whole range of means available for you: my images, Divine music, prayers, and Rosaries. Everything capable of elevating your consciousness and raising it over the commotion reigning in your world will bring you closer to the Path of Light that is awaiting you and that will unfold itself before your eyes as soon as you prepare yourselves.

It is impossible for you to continue wandering in the dark. It is necessary to come out to the Path of Light, the Divine Path.

Stop blaming other people, other countries and nations, your governments and state structures for your troubles and misfortune. Everything surrounding you corresponds to your level of consciousness. Change your consciousness, harmonize it with God, and everything in your lives will change within the lifetime of one generation.

I am telling you that the Divine Light opportunity is within hailing distance, yet you do not see it. You need to illuminate the space around you with the Divine Light emanating from the innermost depths of your being, and then you will obtain the understanding and knowledge that are necessary for you in order to come out of the darkness into the Light.

I have come to you today to remind you that everything is possible with God. And your aspiration for the Common Weal and Good will be supported by all the Heavens and the energies of the coming New Age.

You need not grieve and inflame the passions of despair. I am telling you that the end of darkness is coming, and only Light is ahead of you!

I AM Mother Mary, loving all of you and caring for you.

Let God into your life

Mother Mary
June 23, 2013

I AM Mother Mary.

I have come. What do you think we are going to talk about today?

I think that there are many things that you would like to discuss with me and many questions that you would like to ask me. However, I have not come in order to have a quiet talk today. I am in a decisive mood and ready for a serious talk that we will be having.

I would like to talk to you about your service and your obligations. Before coming into this incarnation, many of you have assumed many obligations upon yourselves related to your service for the world. Yet, by now you have forgotten what you have taken upon yourselves. And this is sorrowful. It is especially sorrowful now when the situation on the planet is still worsening, when darkness is obscuring people's eyes and making it impossible to take a deep breath and aspire toward bright and joyful energies of regeneration.

First of all, I am speaking to the people of my dear Russia. But I am also ready to talk with many of my beloved children scattered around the globe.

I am happy when we combine our efforts together in a joint prayer for peace in the world. And I am sad when the rows of those involved in the prayers thin out, when momentary entrainment distracts you from the main thing: the prayerful opposition against any negative forces and manifestations of your world.

Together in our prayers we are able to change any situation in any country of the world. Together in our joint prayers we can reverse even the most difficult situation and direct it into an easy and joyous Divine flow.

I am ready to stay with you in your prayer. I am ready to join the people who appeal to me in their heartfelt prayers and ask for help.

God gives you unprecedented opportunities. God is ready to come to every aspiring person during sincere prayer. And together with Him I will stay with each of you.

I am craving for the moment of your sincere prayer in order to come and to reinforce it. Sometimes I come to those of you who have assumed the obligations upon themselves to read my Rosaries every day. And how surprised and disappointed I am when instead of prayer you plunge into other things that seem more important for you. I come exactly at the time of your prayer in order to strengthen it and to pray with you. I cannot find you, and this is very sad.

Beloved, do not upset me with your inconsistency and laziness. Do understand that now your prayers can only save and improve the situation that has been formed in Russia and in the world. Only with your prayers you can prevent the most terrible thing.

I am asking you. I am begging you.

Beloved, it is not hard, is it? Even when you do not have time to read a Rosary, just simply aspire to me with all the love of your heart. I will meet your eyes and understand that you remember me, though the circumstances do not allow you to spare the time for praying that day. I will come to you the next day, and together we will contribute our prayerful efforts for the Common Good.

The power of our joint prayers is reinforced now as never before. And I assure you that we can prevent the most terrible consequences of any incorrect actions of people in the past and present if we oppose the negative energies with our faith and unity.

Imagine a mighty prayer wheel that is rolling from one side of Earth to the other end. Imagine how the faithful voices of those who are praying merge into one loud voice. And this voice is heard everywhere on Earth.

Together we will be able to withstand!

I am telling you that the situation is so difficult that it is hard to believe it. And the only thing that I am asking you for now is to give me the energy of your prayers so that I can allocate the energy according to my view.

Entrust your prayerful efforts to me. Ask me for help and I will send my angels to help in those situations that seem unsolvable.

Imagine that my angels and I enter the walls of your government bodies. By our presence we will transform the situation and create the preponderance of the forces during any decision-making.

Imagine me during any negotiations that are taking place at the government level, as if I were also sitting at the negotiating table, and I will supervise any decision-making in your world whether it concerns politics, the economy, education, health care, culture, or social welfare. Your visualizations and prayers will allow me and other Ascended Masters to be involved in decision-making at any national level. Thanks to such a simple practice we can reverse any situation and direct its settlement along the Divine Path.

I know that many people are now suffering from depression, and I know that the hearts of many people are held captive by fear and hatred.

Beloved, all this happens because of the lack of God's presence in your lives. The Divine energy is blocked not only by you yourselves but also with the help of mass media, which immerses you in negative states of consciousness.

Only the flow of Divine energy that you attract during your prayer can purify your bodies, your consciousness and subconsciousness, and forever liberate you from fear, depression, and hatred. Any imperfect state of your consciousness can be dissolved by the Divine energy that you will daily attract into your life with the help of your prayers.

I will stay with every one of you during your prayers. I will strengthen the influence of your prayers, and I will help you. But I cannot do anything for you unless you give me the energy of your prayers and the energy of your love that you send to me while meditating on my image.

Therefore, do not blame anyone if you experience negative states of consciousness, if troubles and misfortunes dim your eyes. God is so merciful that one prayer or one fervent appeal can be enough to change any situation.

You must manifest all your prayers and appeals only in the name of God.

We will be able to change any situation! We will do it! The Divine miracle is beside you. It is ready to be manifested, but the energy of your prayers and of your positive aspirations toward happiness, bliss, and good is needed to manifest the miracle.

You get what you strive for. If every day you argue about everything, if you criticize your government, all the people around you, and God himself, then you will hardly achieve a positive result, and it is unlikely that you will ever be happy in your lives.

If you are able to sustain faith and love in your hearts no matter what, if you are ready to protect yourselves and your nearest and dearest by your prayers and love, then the worst and irreparable things will go past you and your families and friends. And if from year to year there are more and more people who accept the priority of God and His Law, then no difficulties, no calamities or crises, can threaten your country and its people.

You can see that God always looks after you.

Let God into your life.

I AM Mother Mary.

You should apply maximum effort to return God into your life

Mother Mary
December 24, 2013

I AM Mother Mary.

I have come to you today to show you the omens of a better life and the better fate that awaits the sons and daughters of God on planet Earth.

Now there is very little sun in the northern hemisphere, and only hope warms peoples' souls. You know that some time will pass and the sun will start rising above the horizon, higher and higher every day.

It is the same way in your spiritual life: The twilight of your human consciousness will inevitably be replaced by a bright sunny day. The sun of your Divinity should illuminate your mind and all your thoughts and feelings. And this will happen, beloved.

Now the dark forces and energies are raging in your world. And each person transmitting the light energy into your world is exposed to censure and even persecution. And this is very sorrowful.

Some time ago, my son Jesus experienced the manifestation of human hatred and hostility to the fullest extent. He devoted his life to serving others. Many incurably ill people were healed by Him with God's help. Many people came to see the miracles performed by my son Jesus.

However, the more that He did for the people, the greater was the opposition that formed and grew stronger against Him and His mission.

In terms of human logic, it is very difficult to explain what happened when the frenzied crowd, which included the people healed by Jesus, furiously demanded the execution of my son.

However, if we allow ourselves to rise to a higher level of consciousness, then that sorrowful event of Christ's crucifixion will become clear. Jesus brought a huge amount of Light to the world, and it is not only the light of knowledge but also a huge amount of Divine energy.

On the subconscious level, everything that was not from the Light felt an aversion to the mission of Christ. This aversion was the manifestation of the forces opposite to the Light. You know the law: For every action there is an equal and opposite counter-action. This law of the physical world is entirely applicable to the spiritual processes taking place in the world. If a person has the potential to bring the Divine light into the illusory world, then he will face the opposition of the forces that stand for the illusion.

This is so, beloved. And this law still keeps working in your world.

By the example of Jesus Christ, many generations of Christians had the opportunity to study the work of this law. Many true followers of Christianity, the followers of the essence of the Teachings of Christ but not of the letter, still experience the pressure of the opposing forces.

This confrontation in your world is inevitable and cannot stop at once. Like everything in your world, the confrontation between the two main forces acting in the Universe cannot instantly stop. But, in the course of time, this opposition must become less destructive. In the distant future, these two forces will be balanced in their manifestation to such an extent that collaboration and cooperation will arise from this confrontation.

Many of you, beloved, confront each other. It happens even when you seem to follow the same spiritual path.

This confrontation is explained by the imperfection of your world. Therefore, the two opposite forces manifest themselves through your beings. At this stage, this manifestation represents animosity, suspicion, and even hatred. One and the same person can fall under the influence of different forces during the day.

Beloved, all this happens because of the lack of Love in your hearts. And the lack of Love in your hearts is caused by the isolation of your world from the world of the Divine.

No God, no Love. Therefore, you should apply the maximum effort to return God into your life.

Look at everything that is around you in your world: advertisements, urban landscapes, gloomy faces of passers-by, and TV programs. Your world is not a friendly one. And always staying in the states of fear, tension, and gloom, people absorb these states of the outer world. Even the youth in their early years lose the charge of optimism and joy that should be characteristic of a young person.

The true joys are being replaced by substitutes: the surrogates of movies, music, and drugs.

True Love is being replaced by surrogate love that has nothing in common with the great feeling of Love.

While staying in the non-divine external environment, it is very easy to lose your soul. Your time is dangerous for the souls of many people who are in embodiment and especially for the youth. This is why the other Masters and I come to you: to give you an understanding of the processes taking place in your world, to remind you that the world was not always so unfortunate, and that a bright future awaits humanity.

First, this future will germinate in the hearts of a few people who possess a strong Spirit and can oppose the surrounding illusion with their faith and devotion to God and the Masters. Later, when there are more of these souls that have the Divine state of consciousness, humanity in its majority will start turning to the Light. And people having the state of consciousness that most of humanity currently have, will be considered exceptional black sheep who require unlimited Compassion and Love.

Only under the influence of Compassion, Mercy, and Love, the souls of many of you can stretch the spiritual folds of your garments and rise up to Life.

The feat of my son Jesus was in the fact that He continued to feel Love toward the people who tortured Him and were out for His death.

That is exactly why millions of Christians all over the world continue to worship the feat of my son.

I foresee that in the future many of those who are now reading this Message of mine will be able to respond with Love to all the traps and tricks of the illusory forces. And even in the face of death, my children can show Mercy and Compassion to the souls of those who torture them, for many people know not what they do. If they knew, they would never allow themselves to carry out many of their deeds.

You can show the Path to many lost souls. Do pray for the insight of humanity and forgive everyone.

I AM Mother Mary.

Always stay in Love, and everything will start changing around you

Beloved Mother Mary
December 23, 2014

I AM Mother Mary, having come to you.

Today, I would like to talk to you about your needs and your necessities of the hour. Many of you turn to me for help. I can render my help to many of you.

However, there are a certain number of souls who are so burdened with the unnecessary load of their past sins, that I wish I could but I cannot render them my help. My angels and I are constantly in a state of service and special attention to your requests and appeals.

I must tell you that even when the help cannot be given in all fullness, we do everything possible in order to alleviate your sufferings.

The tears of repentance that I often see in your eyes during our conversation tell me much more about you than your words and even your prayers.

You cannot imagine what kind of work the Ascended Hosts have to do in order to enable your souls to realize many of your sins and to repent for them.

When repentance comes into your heart, your karmic burden becomes easier by half. And you can dissolve the remaining half by your daily prayers and efforts aimed at relieving the plight of other suffering souls.

Believe me that your help to the suffering souls is invaluable in your time.

Many people do not even realize that they are suffering. They cannot understand this because they have nothing to compare their state with. They are so burdened with their problems and concerns that they do not see even a gleam of Light in the total darkness of their surrounding life.

So, give the ray of hope to these souls. Open your hearts to Love, and send a small part of your Love to each suffering heart in your world.

This will not be hard for you, will it? This will not be difficult for you, to warm the violent hearts of politicians, economists, government officials, and commercial structures with your Love, will it? After all, you can overcome the stereotypes within yourself and see in the most (in your opinion) malicious and ossified government and business officials, the hearts of people who just do not know Love.

Many people have fallen under the spell of the illusory forces.

They are sleeping and are having horrible dreams, and they try to promote their dreams into their lives.

This is because there is no God or His manifestation, Love, in the hearts of those people. The lack of God is exactly the thing that makes many politicians do horrible deeds. If someone's Love could warm their hearts with at least a short impulse of Goodness and Light, we predict that many horrible consequences of their actions could be prevented because they will change. The impulse of Divine energy can dissolve fear and aggression in the hearts of the most hardened criminals and God-haters.

It happens sometimes that at a particular moment a person wakens from his dream, and tears of repentance appear on his cheeks. The repentant person can no longer cause harm to others, to children and elderly people.

Therefore, do take the trouble to grow Love in your heart at this dark time and send this Love to those who, in your opinion, need this Love so that the hearts of those people can change. This way we will be able to change the future of the whole planet by our mutual efforts, no matter how sad and joyless the future may seem.

We can change any situation on planet Earth by our mutual efforts.

I am urging you not to be lazy and to improve yourself and those imperfections that are still blocking the manifestation of Divine Love in your hearts.

Think about what is preventing your hearts from manifesting Love.

Think about how to dissolve the ice of fear, aggression, and lack of faith that literally fetters your hearts.

Think about what you can do for other people — not only for your relatives but also for all those people on whom public opinion depends.

Sometimes, one person who has enough influence on society can change public opinion to overcome the negative tendencies in the world.

You must be firm in your faith, and with your faith you will be able to let so much Love into your world that the hearts of many people will change.

Everything can be changed, beloved.

Everything is possible with God's help, absolutely everything. You just need to focus all your efforts on God, His presence in your lives, and His guidance in all your deeds and actions.

Every day and from day to day.

Do not think about those who have forgotten God and show not the best human qualities. Think about Divine Love that is growing in your heart from day to day.

Always stay in Love, and everything will start changing around you.

If you lack faith and devotion, remember me. Remember those quiet minutes when you were able to catch My eye or look at My image and get an answer to your question.

Remember those moments of peaceful joy during our direct communication that you experienced in your life from time to time.

Beloved, I am always with you!

We are together!

I share all your misfortunes and sufferings with you completely, and I do everything possible to alleviate them fully.

May peace, calmness, and goodness always be with you.

I AM Mother Mary, loving you and taking care of you.

The prayer to Most Holy Mother of God

In the name of I AM THAT I AM Most Holy Mother of God, beloved Mother Mary, I pray on bended knee to you.

Words fail me to express the depth of Love in my heart that I feel toward you. Please accept my Love and gratitude.

You know what is most important for the growth of my soul at present. I am asking for your help and support. I ask you to help me not to forget in the midst of the hustle of the day about those quiet minutes of our commune which my soul remembers.

May my unbreakable bond with you support me in my life and help me not to forget about the Higher Path that I intend to follow in this life.

Mother Mary
January 4, 2009

About the author

Tatyana Nicholaevna Mickushina was born in the south of western Siberia in the town of Omsk. During all of her life, she has been praying and asking God to grant her an opportunity to work for Him.

In 2004, Tatyana N. Mickushina was granted a Messenger's Mantle of the Great White Brotherhood and received an opportunity to bring the Words of the Masters to people. Since 2005, at certain periods of time, she receives messages from the Ascended Masters in a special way. With the help of many people, the messages have been translated into English and many other languages so that more people can become familiar with them.

"The only thing the Ascended Masters want is to spread their Teaching throughout the world.

The Masters give their messages with the feeling of great Love. Love has no limits.

There are no boundaries between the hearts of people living in different countries; there are no boundaries between the worlds. The boundaries exist only in the consciousness of people.

The Masters appeal through me to every person living on planet Earth.

I wish you success on the spiritual Path!"

Light and Love!

Tatyana Mickushina

WORDS OF WISDOM SERIES

The "Words of Wisdom" series of books was created based on the Ascended Masters' Messages that have been given through T.N. Mickushina. Since 2005, she has received over 450 Messages from more than 50 Beings of Light. You can find the Dictations on the website "Sirius" **sirius-eng.net** (English version) and **sirius-ru.net** or **sirius-net.org** (Russian version).

The Ascended Masters have been communicating with mankind for thousands of years. Since ancient times, the Masters of Shambala were known in the East. In different teachings, people call them by different names: the Teachers of Humanity, the Ascended Masters, the Masters of Wisdom or the Great White Brotherhood.

These Teachers have reached the next evolutionary step in their development and continue their development in the Higher planes. These Higher Beings consider it Their duty to help humanity in the development of their consciousness.

The method which the Ascended Masters have chosen to communicate with humanity is the transmission of the Messages (Dictations) that are written by the Messenger who can use a special method to provide the perception of the Messages from the higher, etheric octaves of Light.

The first Dictation from Sanat Kumara on March 4, 2005, gave us the following message:

"I AM Sanat Kumara and I have come today to inform the world about a new opportunity and a new dispensation which the Heavens have decided to free through our new Russian Messenger Tatyana.

This turn of events will be unexpected for many of you. Many of you will experience contradictory feelings while reading this message.

However, we do not want to force anybody to believe or not to believe the things to be told. Our task is to give you this knowledge. Its acceptance is a matter of your own free will.

Times have changed and the New Age has come. The worlds have converged. Things which seemed to be an impossible dream a few years ago, even last year, are starting to become real now. We are getting an opportunity to speak through many of you and we are using this opportunity."

MASTERS OF WISDOM SERIES

Each of the Masters of Wisdom strives to give us what they consider most vital at the present moment of transition. Every message contains the energies of different Masters who give those messages. The Masters speak about the current historical moment on planet Earth. They tell us about energy and vibrations, about the illusion of this world and about the Divine Reality, about the Higher Self of a human and about his lower bodies. They give us concrete recommendations on exactly how to change our own consciousness and continue on the evolutionary Path. It is recommended that you prepare yourself for reading every message very carefully. You have to tune to the Master who is giving the message with the help of proper music, with the help of the Master's image, or by using a prayer or a meditation before reading the message. That way you align your energies, elevate your consciousness, and the messages can benefit you.

SAINT GERMAIN

SAINT GERMAIN

Saint Germain is at present an Ascended Master, the Hierarch of the New Age. In his last incarnation as the Count de Saint Germain in the 18th century, he exerted a great influence on the course of world history. The Messages of Master Saint Germain are charged with optimism and faith in the forthcoming Golden Age! He teaches about preparing for a New Age by transforming our consciousness, and reminds us: "Joy and Love come to you when your Faith is steadfast, when you rely in your consciousness on God and the Ascended Hosts."

SANAT KUMARA

SANAT KUMARA

Masters of Wisdom, first of all Sanat Kumara, remind us about our Divine origin and call us to wake up to a Higher reality, because Divine Reality by its love, wisdom, and beauty exceeds any of the most wonderful aspects of our physical world. The Messages of Sanat Kumara include Teachings on true and false messengers, Communities of the Holy Spirit, responsibility for the duties that one has taken upon him/herself before their incarnation, the right use of the money energy, the choice of everyone between the Eternal and the perishable world, overcoming the ego, the Path of Initiations, and many other topics

MORYA

MORYA

Messages from the Teacher, Master Morya, have been given through Helena Blavatsky in the 19th century, Helena and Nicholas Roerich in the period around 1920-1950, and Mark and Elizabeth Clare Prophet in the 1960's. Master Morya is still actively working on the Spiritual plane to help the humanity of the World.

Now the Masters continue their work through a Messenger from Russia, Tatyana Mickushina.

This book contains selected Messages from Master Morya. Many Teachings are given in the Messages, including the Teachings about the correct actions on the physical plane, Service to Brotherhood, the attainment of the qualities of a disciple such as devotion, persistence, aspiration, and discipline. Some aspects of the Teaching about changing of consciousness are also introduced here.

SHIVA

SHIVA

The present volume contains selected Messages of Lord Shiva. Many Teachings are given in these Messages; including the Teaching about God, the Teaching about Discernment of reality from illusion: which helps to ascend to a new level of consciousness and also new aspects of the Guru-chela relationship are considered.

Author page of T. N. Mickushina on Amazon:

amazon.com/author/tatyana_mickushina

OTHERS BOOKS BY TATYANA N. MICKUSHINA

About Yoga and Meditation

A Lecture at a Session of the University of Life Ethics by T. N. Mickushina March 27, 2015 (Materials to the seminars) .

This book is based on the audio recorded lecture by Tatyana N. Mickushina at the University of Life Ethics on March 27, 2015. This lecture explains why so few people can master the practice of true meditation and what those who cannot engage in meditation practice can do.

Treasures of Divine Wisdom

The multivolume book, Words of Wisdom by Tatyana Mickushina, has several thousand pages of text. This book was created to meet the spiritual needs of busy people who are unable to spend much time reading. The book includes the most concise and significant quotations from the book Words of Wisdom.

Masters of Wisdom

MOTHER MARY

Dictations received through the Messenger Tatyana Nicholaevna Mickushina (from 2005 through 2014)

Tatyana N. Mickushina

Websites:

http://sirius-eng.net (English version)
http://sirius-ru.net (Russian version)

Books by T.N.Mickushina on amazon.com:
amazon.com/author/tatyana_mickushina

CPSIA information can be obtained
at www.ICGtesting.com
Printed in the USA
FSHW021950220720
72398FS

9 781973 908289